MAP YOUR PLANET

HABITATS

RACHEL MINAY

Cavendish Square

Published in 2024 by Cavendish Square Publishing, LLC
2544 Clinton Street, Buffalo, NY 14224

Website: cavendishsq.com

Editor: Rachel Minay
Series designer: Rocket Design (East Anglia) Ltd

The publisher would like to thank the following for permission to reproduce their pictures:
Alamy: ITAR-TASS News Agency 13(b); Getty: hstiver 7(b), andreaskrappweis 14(cr), mantaphoto 26(b), Leeman 29(c); NASA (images made by Reto Stockli, NASA's Earth Observatory Team, using data provided by the MODIS Land Science Team) 15(t); Sally Ride EarthKAM 25(b); Shutterstock: Ondrej Prosicky cover (inset), evenfh cover (main), robert mcgillivray 4(c), A7880S 4(b), Rudmer Zwerver 5(c), Christian Roberts-Olsen 5(b), GUDKOV ANDREY 6(b), HTU 7(t), Vlad61 7(c), Tarpan 8(l), Designua 8–9, Melissa Leitner 9(t), Dennis W Donohue 9(b), Andrei Stepanov 10(t), David Havel 11(tr), Paul Loewen 11(bl), evgenii mitroshin 12(l), longtaildog 12(r), Danny Ye 13(t), Stephan Morris 14(b), Rich Carey 15(c), Katesalin Pagkaihang 15(b), Zhukova Valentyna 16(c), Paul Roedding 16(b), Ryan.R.Smith.87 17(r), Francois Gagnon 18(b), TommyBrison 19(c), Aureliy 19(b), Maggy Meyer 20(c), Vaganundo_Che 20(b), GUDKOV ANDREY 21(t), Alina Lavrenova 21(b), Nicholas Taffs 22(c), Nino Weg 23(t), Armin Rose 23(b), Cat Downie 24(bl), Jose HERNANDEZ Camera 51 24(br), Patrick Poendl 25(t), Aqua Images 27(t), cristalvi 27(b), tristan tan 28(t), Na-Me 28(b), Phuong D.Nguyen 29(b).
Design elements by Shutterstock.
Map illustrations: Julian Baker: 12–13, 17, 20–21, 24–25, 29.

Cataloging-in-Publication Data

Names: Minay, Rachel.
Title: Habitats / Rachel Minay.
Description: New York : Cavendish Square Publishing, 2024. | Series: Map your planet | Includes glossary and index.
Identifiers: ISBN 9781502668448 (pbk.) | ISBN 9781502668455 (library bound) | ISBN 9781502668462 (ebook)
Subjects: LCSH: Habitat (Ecology)--Juvenile literature. | Habitat conservation--Juvenile literature. | Adaptation (Biology)--Juvenile literature.
Classification: LCCQH541.14 M563 2024 | DDC 577--dc23

CPSIA compliance information: Batch #CSCSQ24:
For further information contact Cavendish Square Publishing LLC at 1-877-980-4450.

Printed in the United States of America

Find us on

CONTENTS

WHAT IS A HABITAT?

A habitat is a place where an animal or plant lives. Living things rely on their habitats to find food, shelter, and a mate so they can reproduce.

ADAPTATION

Animals and plants are adapted to their habitats. For example, a dolphin's streamlined shape helps it swim through its watery habitat, while a desert cactus does not need a lot of water to survive.

These penguins are adapted for their freezing Antarctic habitat. They have thick skin with lots of blubber (fat) to help keep warm, and webbed feet for strong swimming.

MAP MASTERS

This map shows a range of plants and animals and the places they live around the world.

ECOSYSTEMS

An ecosystem is a community of animals and plants, together with their habitat. The living things in an ecosystem rely on each other to survive, as well as on the nonliving things, such as water and soil.

HABITAT LOSS

Habitat loss causes serious problems for wildlife. Habitats can be:

destroyed – for example by people clearing land for farming or by natural causes, such as flooding

spoiled or damaged – for example by pollution

fragmented – for example by road-building or natural disasters, such as a volcanic eruption. Habitat fragmentation separates species and means animals have a smaller area to hunt and find a mate in.

Roads often break up habitats, but in some places people build wildlife bridges or underpasses to allow animals to move safely from one side to the other.

Fire can destroy or fragment habitats. It can have both natural and human causes.

TYPES OF HABITAT

Our planet is a rich patchwork of different habitats, from tiny rock pools and freezing mountaintops to vast tropical rain forests and cities filled with people.

LAND HABITATS

There are many different land habitats. Rain forests are important because they have the most biodiversity, which means the greatest variety of species in an area. Other examples of land habitats are deserts, grasslands, and mountains.

Mountain gorillas live in mountain forests in central Africa. They are endangered due to habitat loss and poaching, but conservation means numbers are rising.

WATER HABITATS

Water habitats can be salty, such as the sea, or fresh, such as rivers and lakes. Earth is a "blue planet" – two-thirds of it is covered by ocean – so many species live in saltwater habitats. Freshwater makes up only around 2 percent of Earth's surface, but it is vital. We all need freshwater to survive, and it also provides biodiverse habitats.

The common kingfisher likes a habitat with clear water and riverbank trees or shrubs. It perches on an overhanging branch, swooping down when it spots its prey.

Coral reefs are such biodiverse saltwater habitats, they are sometimes called "rainforests of the sea."

URBAN HABITATS

Most people in the world live in cities, but it's easy to forget that cities provide habitats for wildlife too. As urban expansion squeezes out traditional habitats, many animals have adapted to urban life.

Peregrine falcons have adapted to life in cities, where they hunt urban birds, such as pigeons, and nest in high buildings.

MAPPING GLOBAL BIOMES

A biome is a big area that shares a similar climate and landscape. There are many habitats within each biome.

1 ICE AND POLAR DESERT

The white areas of the map around the Arctic and Antarctic are solid ice sheets. Most life here is found around the coasts where animals can find food in the ocean.

Antarctica contains the most hostile habitats on Earth. Weddell seals live and give birth on the ice, and dive to find food in the sea.

2 MEDITERRANEAN

The Mediterranean biome has dry summers and rainy winters. It is found around the Mediterranean Sea, but also in parts of California in the U.S., Chile, South Africa, and Australia.

Plants such as olive trees and lavender can withstand the long, dry summers of their Mediterranean habitat.

Living things have to be hardy to survive in montane climates. The snow leopard has thick fur and broad paws that help it to walk on the snow of its cold, mountain habitat.

3 MONTANE

Montane habitats are found on mountain slopes and include forests, grasslands, and alpine tundra. They are often at high altitude and in a cold climate.

TUNDRA

Tundra is a very cold habitat found near the North Pole. The animals and plants that make their homes here have to cope with extreme conditions.

TREELESS TUNDRA

Tundra has a permanently frozen layer of soil called permafrost. It is very hard for trees to grow here – in fact, the word "tundra" comes from a word meaning "treeless plain." Arctic tundra is found in northern Europe, Russia, Canada, Alaska, and Greenland. Alpine tundra lies farther south on high mountains above the tree line. Although most of Antarctica is polar desert, there is also some Antarctic tundra.

Cold temperatures and a short growing season mean only low-growing plants can survive in the tundra, including grasses, mosses, and low shrubs.

WILDLIFE

Many animals of the tundra, including the Arctic fox and the snowy owl, have white fur or feathers to blend in with the snow. Others, such as the musk ox, have thick, long hair to help keep them warm in their cold tundra habitat.

SURVIVING THE WINTER

Many mammals and birds migrate to avoid the long, hard tundra winter. Few use hibernation, because the ground is too frozen to dig up. One animal that does is the Arctic ground squirrel, which lines its shallow burrow with leaves and musk ox hair to hibernate for seven months or more.

The Arctic tern has two summers a year! It breeds in summer in the northern tundra and migrates to Antarctica for the southern summer.

FACT

THE ARCTIC TERN'S 43,500-MILE (70,000 KM) ROUND TRIP IS THE LONGEST MIGRATION OF ANY ANIMAL ON EARTH.

snowy owl

musk ox

Animals that stay in the tundra in winter need good adaptations to survive. The thick fur of the Arctic hare is gray in summer but turns snow-white in winter to provide camouflage.

MAPPING NORTHERN RUSSIA

As the world's largest country by area, Russia covers a number of biomes and habitats, including taiga forest (see page 14) and steppe grasslands (see page 19). The northern coast is tundra.

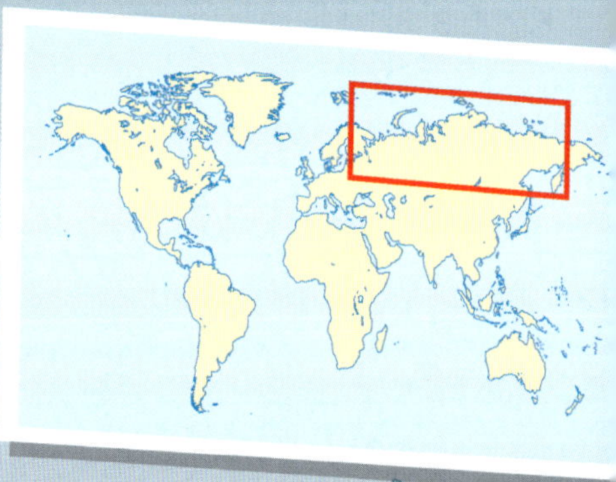

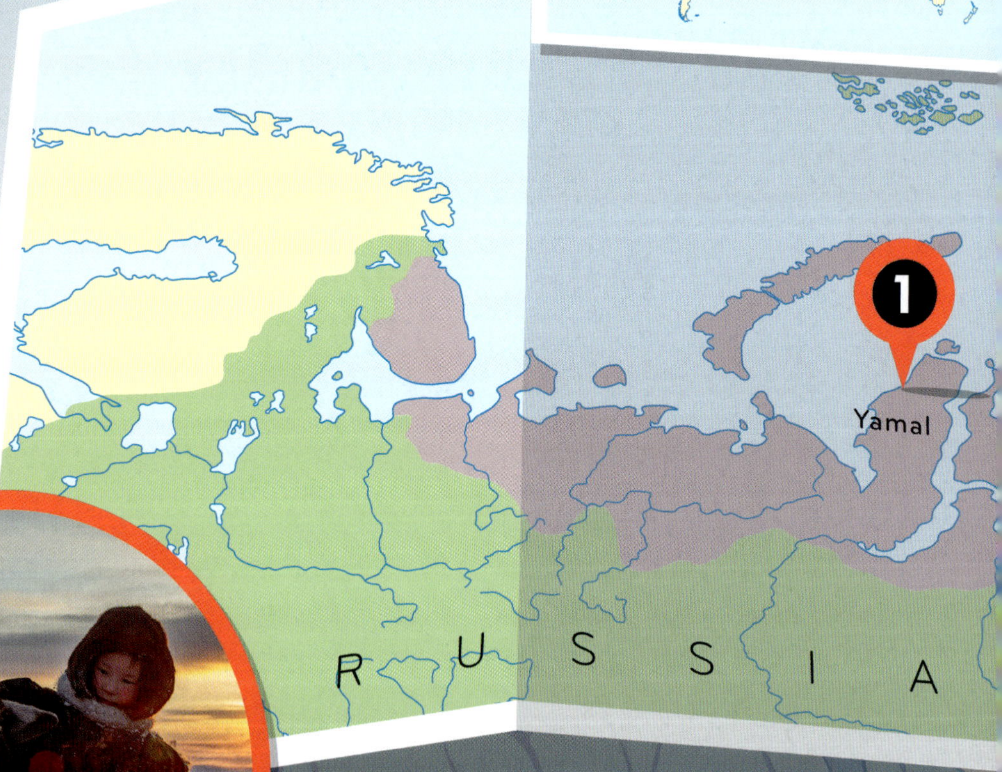

1 YAMAL PENINSULA

The tundra is home to people, as well as wildlife. The Nenets are indigenous people, many of whom are nomadic reindeer herders. They migrate north to summer pastures, and return south in winter.

Reindeer dig through the snow to feed on lichen. When the lichen runs out, they move on.

2 TAYMYR PENINSULA

Musk ox were once spread across northern Russia, but became extinct on the Taymyr Peninsula about 2,500 years ago. They were successfully reintroduced in the 1970s.

From 30 animals in the 1970s, by 2010 there were around 6,500 musk ox on the Taymyr Peninsula.

RIVER DELTAS

There are a range of habitats within a biome. The river deltas of the northeastern Russian tundra, including the Lena, the Yana, and the Indigirka, are major breeding grounds for migratory birds.

The spectacled eider is a sea duck that breeds in wet tundra habitats, such as the Indigirka Delta.

FACT

IN 2007, A NENETS REINDEER HERDER FOUND A WOOLLY MAMMOTH ALMOST PERFECTLY PRESERVED IN THE PERMAFROST OF THE YAMAL PENINSULA.

Nicknamed Lubya, this baby mammoth lived an incredible 40,000 years ago!

FORESTS

Forests are habitats made up of trees and other woody plants. There are different kinds of forests around the world, and they are important for the planet as well as its wildlife.

TAIGA

The world's largest land biome is taiga, which is also known as boreal or snow forest. The trees in taiga habitats are mostly evergreen and coniferous, such as pine, fir, and spruce.

The Siberian tiger lives in both taiga and mixed forest habitats, where it feeds on elk, deer, and wild boar.

FACT

FOREST HABITATS CONTAIN AROUND 80 PERCENT OF ALL BIODIVERSITY FOUND ON LAND.

MIXED AND DECIDUOUS FOREST

Sometimes called temperate forest, these habitats have a mild climate that has definite seasons and a distinct winter. Deciduous trees are ones that lose their leaves in winter, such as oak, beech, and maple.

Deciduous forests contain plants, such as bluebells, that flower before the trees grow their leaves in spring. Birds, such as tawny owls, also like this habitat. They nest in the hollows of old trees.

TROPICAL RAIN FOREST

Tropical rain forests occur near the equator, where the temperature is warm and doesn't change much throughout the year. There are usually two seasons – rainy and dry. Rain forest habitats have the greatest diversity of species on the planet, but they are threatened by deforestation.

MAP MASTERS

Forests are vital to the planet's health because they soak up carbon dioxide (CO_2) and make oxygen. The green areas on these satellite maps show how good the world's forests are at taking in CO_2 – taiga takes in lots of CO_2 in June and July, while rain forests take in lots all year.

February 2016

July 2016

palm oil plantation

HABITAT LOSS

Orangutans live in rain forests, but much of their habitat has been destroyed to grow palm oil. All three species of orangutans are critically endangered.

MAPPING THE AMERICAS

North America is mostly in the northern hemisphere and South America in the southern. A map of both continents shows a range of climates and forest habitats.

1 CANADIAN BOREAL FOREST

Canada is divided into eight forest regions, of which the boreal forest is the largest – about 80 percent of the total.

Canada's boreal region also contains many mountain, lake, river, and wetland habitats.

2 NEW ENGLAND DECIDUOUS FOREST

The temperate deciduous forests of New England are known for their amazing autumn colors.

The black-capped chickadee lives in a deciduous and mixed forest habitat. It is the state bird of Maine and Massachusetts, both in New England.

FACT

AROUND 1,300 BIRD SPECIES, 40,000 PLANT SPECIES, AND 2.5 MILLION INSECT SPECIES LIVE IN THE AMAZON RAIN FOREST.

3 AMAZON RAIN FOREST

The warm, wet Amazon is the most biodiverse place in the world – there are around 16,000 different species of trees alone. Rain forests contain millions of species, some we haven't even discovered yet!

A sloth has specialized hands and feet with long claws. These help it to hang upside down from trees in its rain forest habitat.

GRASSLANDS

There are different types of grasslands, but, as the name suggests, they are all habitats dominated by grasses.

GET TO KNOW GRASSLANDS

Like forests, grasslands can be tropical or temperate, depending on where they are in the world. All grasslands are in places where there is too little rain for many trees to grow.

SAVANNA

Tropical grassland is called savanna. It is always found in warm climates that have a wet season and a dry season. Plants and animals have to adapt to the long dry season, for example animals may migrate long distances to find food and water. Savanna is found in around half of Africa, plus areas of Australia, South America, and India.

The tropical savanna of Australia is a habitat for grass-eating marsupials, such as the eastern gray kangaroo and agile wallaby.

Savanna is grassland scattered with a few trees.

TEMPERATE GRASSLANDS

Temperate grasslands have different names around the world, for example they are called steppes in Asia, plains and prairies in North America, and veldts in South Africa. They are found in places with hot summers and cold winters, and have less rainfall than the savanna. The main plants are grasses, with no trees or shrubs except in some river valleys.

The middle of North America was once covered with prairie grasses and wildflowers. Now, most of the land has been converted for farming – just 1–2 percent of the original prairie habitat remains.

Steppes, such as this area in Kazakhstan, are grasslands with short grasses.

MAPPING THE SERENGETI

The Serengeti is a savanna habitat in East Africa. Beautiful landscapes, diverse wildlife, and an awesome migration make the Serengeti one of the world's most incredible natural wonders.

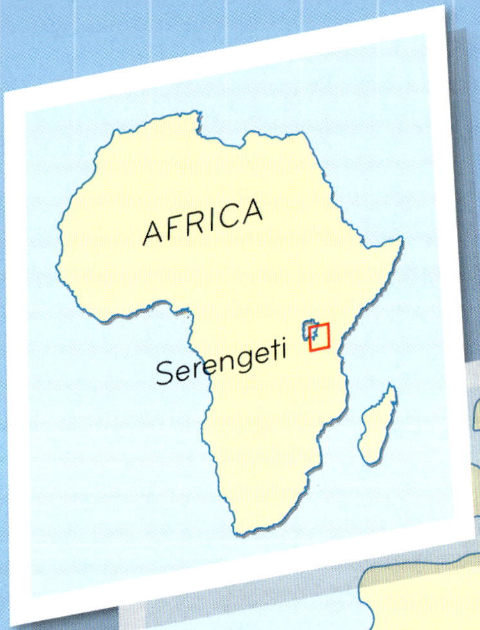

MASS MIGRATION

The Serengeti is well known for its annual migration of wildebeest and other animals. The grassland habitat and the migration are the result of distinct rainy and dry seasons.

1 SOUTHERN PLAINS

The wildebeest feed and give birth on the rain-fed grasslands before they start their epic migration in March. Other hoofed animals also gather here in the wet season, including zebra, impala, and buffalo.

Giraffes can roam the plains in herds of 40 or more.

2 SERONERA RIVER VALLEY

From April to June, the migration has to pass the lions, leopards, and cheetahs of what is called the Big Cat Capital of Africa!

Cheetahs are one of the top predators of the African savanna.

DESERTS

Deserts can be hot or cold, but they all occur in places with little rainfall. Desert animals and plants are specially adapted to live in these extremely dry habitats.

FACT

MIDDAY IN A HOT DESERT OFTEN EXCEEDS 104°F (40°C), BUT TEMPERATURES CAN DROP TO FREEZING AT NIGHT.

HOT AND DRY

Most hot deserts are found close to the equator. They have a distinct summer and winter, but are warm all year – even winter temperatures are 68–86°F (20–30°C). There can be big extremes of temperature between day and night. Typical mammals of these habitats are small, nocturnal burrowers. Large mammals are rare because most cannot store enough water or cope with the heat of the day.

This kangaroo rat burrows into the sandy soil of its Mojave Desert habitat and forages for food in the cool of the night.

Kangaroo rats move by hopping on their big hind legs – which is how they got their name!

Plants in hot deserts are low shrubs and trees. Leaves are small and thick to save water. In cacti the leaves are spines, which also protects the plant from being eaten.

SEMIARID

Semiarid or cold-winter deserts are slightly cooler than hot deserts, and have dry summers and winters. As with hot deserts, animals often stay out of the heat in burrows or move around to stay in the shade of plants.

DESERTS

Deserts can be hot or cold, but they all occur in places with little rainfall. Desert animals and plants are specially adapted to live in these extremely dry habitats.

FACT

MIDDAY IN A HOT DESERT OFTEN EXCEEDS 104°F (40°C), BUT TEMPERATURES CAN DROP TO FREEZING AT NIGHT.

HOT AND DRY

Most hot deserts are found close to the equator. They have a distinct summer and winter, but are warm all year – even winter temperatures are 68–86°F (20–30°C). There can be big extremes of temperature between day and night. Typical mammals of these habitats are small, nocturnal burrowers. Large mammals are rare because most cannot store enough water or cope with the heat of the day.

This kangaroo rat burrows into the sandy soil of its Mojave Desert habitat and forages for food in the cool of the night.

Kangaroo rats move by hopping on their big hind legs – which is how they got their name!

Plants in hot deserts are low shrubs and trees. Leaves are small and thick to save water. In cacti the leaves are spines, which also protect the plant from being eaten.

SEMIARID

Semiarid or cold-winter deserts are slightly cooler than hot deserts, and have dry summers and winters. As with hot deserts, animals often stay out of the heat in burrows or move around to stay in the shade of plants.

COASTAL

Coastal deserts are found in cool to warm regions, and although they are close to the sea they have very little rain – most of the moisture is from fog and dew. These habitats have plants with thick, fleshy leaves or stems that can take in a lot of water and store it. Animal adaptations include toads that seal themselves in burrows for months until there is heavy rainfall.

The Atacama Desert in Chile is the driest place on Earth – some parts have never had any rain! Some people think this dramatic landscape looks like the surface of Mars.

Coastal deserts, like the Atacama, are usually found on the western coastlines of land with mountains to the east.

COLD

We think of deserts as being hot, dry, sandy places, but the two largest deserts in the world are at the poles – the Arctic and Antarctic (see page 8). Cold deserts have short summers and long, cold winters with snow.

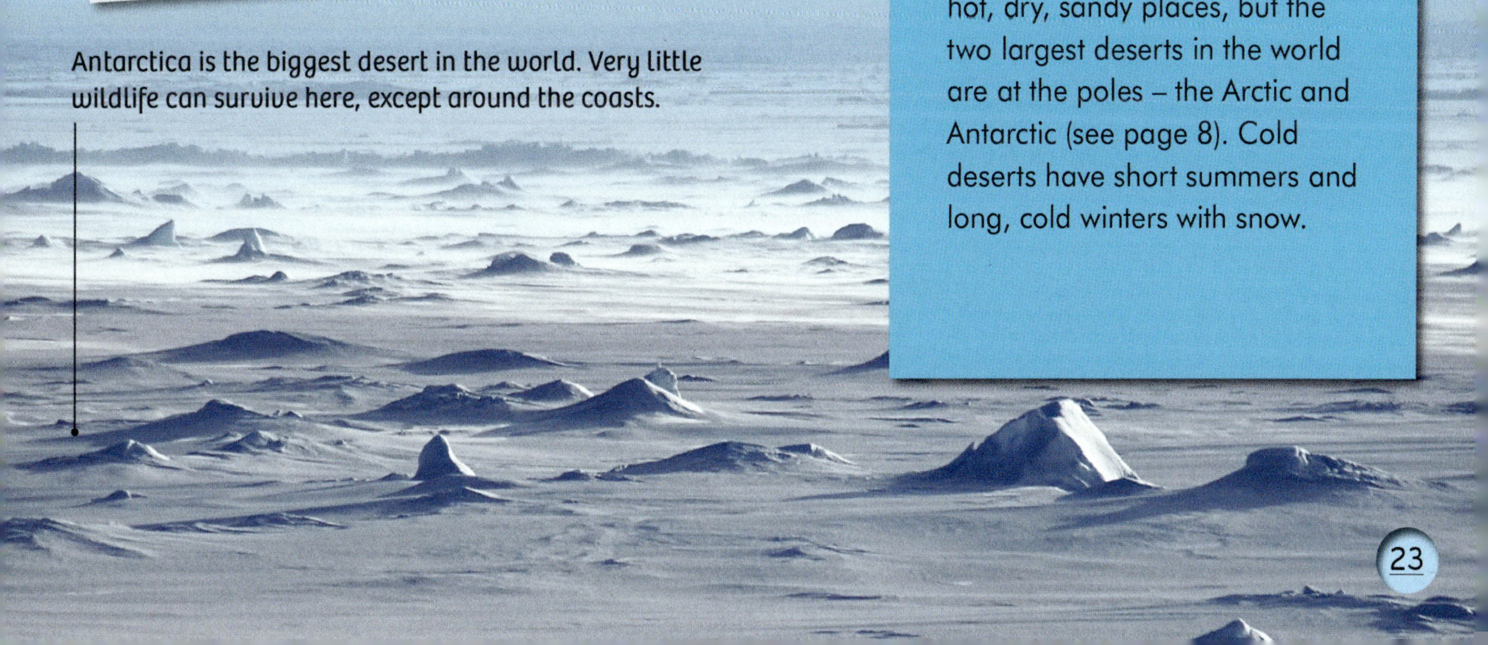

Antarctica is the biggest desert in the world. Very little wildlife can survive here, except around the coasts.

MAPPING THE SAHARA

Stretching right across the top of the African continent, the Sahara is the largest hot desert in the world. How do animals and plants survive in this vast, scorching habitat?

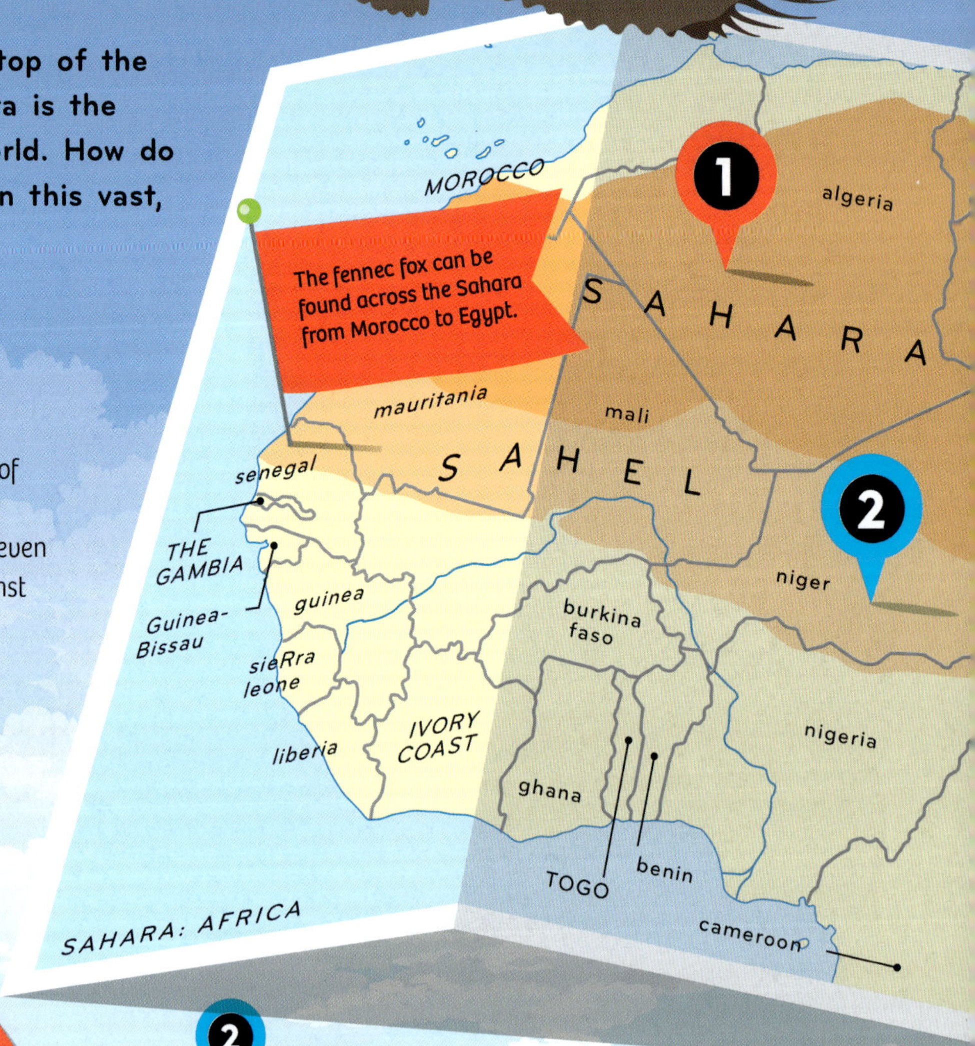

1 FENNEC FOX

The fennec fox digs its den in the sand of its desert habitat. Its large ears radiate heat to keep it cool, while thick hair – even on the soles of its feet – protect it against the burning sun and sand, and keep it warm at night.

The ears, coat, and even kidneys of the fennec fox are all specialized for its hot, low-water habitat.

2 ADDAX

This amazing antelope can live without water for months – or years! It gets hydration from eating plants and saves it in its stomach lining. The addax is critically endangered in the wild due to overhunting, but has a protected habitat on the Termit Massif Reserve in Niger.

The white summer coat of the addax helps to reflect sunlight.

FACT

AT 3.6 MILLION SQUARE MILES (9.2 MILLION SQ KM), THE SAHARA IS A SIMILAR SIZE TO CHINA OR THE U.S.

3 PALM TREES

Palm trees store water in their thick trunks and their wide leaves, or fronds, provide valuable shade for other species. Palm trees can be found across the Sahara, especially around oases.

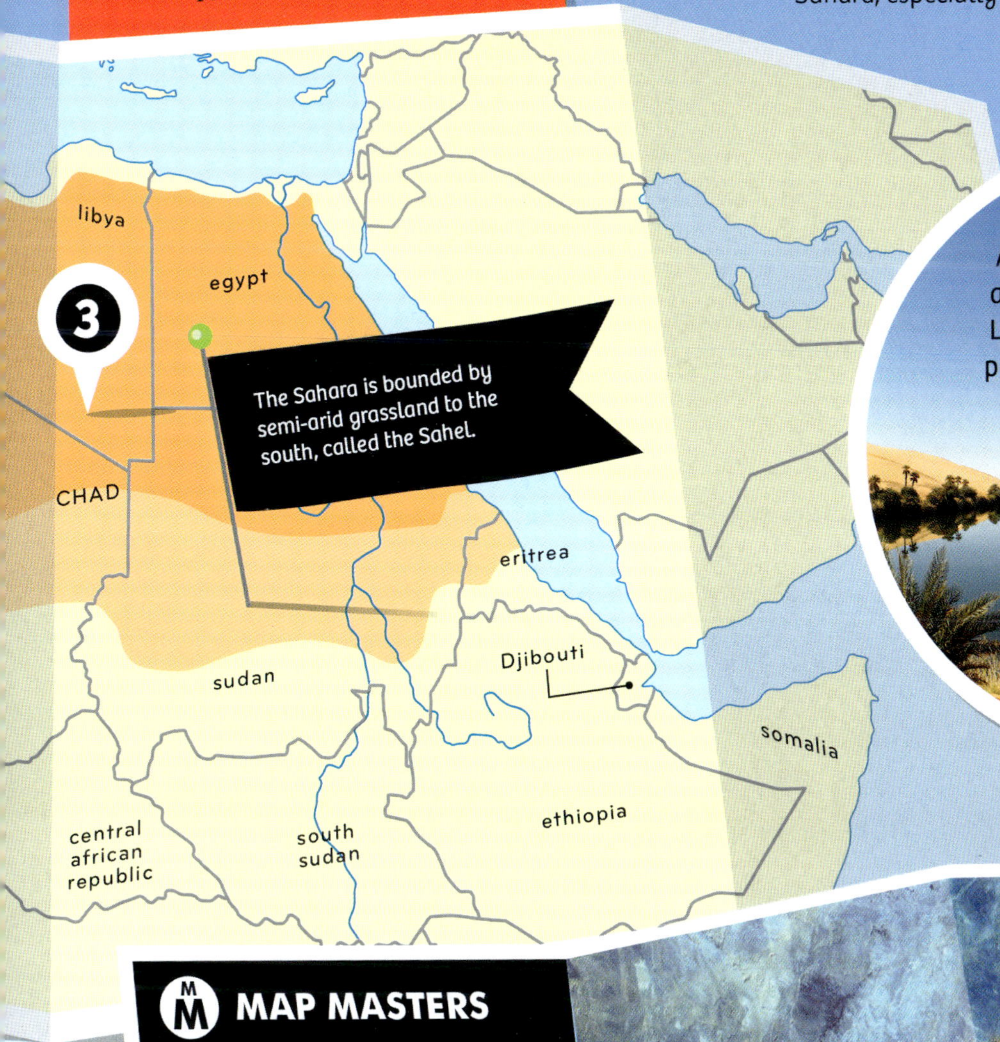

An oasis is a fertile area in a desert. The Ubari lakes in Libya are a habitat for date palms and wetland grasses.

MAP MASTERS

EarthKAM is a NASA project started by Sally Ride, the first U.S. woman in space. Schoolchildren program a camera on the International Space Station and then put their images in context using maps and atlases. Students photographed this beautiful image of the Sahara in western Libya in 2016.

WATER HABITATS

Water habitats include oceans, rivers, wetlands, and more. We know that fish live in water, but these habitats are home to a wide range of animals and plants.

MARINE HABITATS

Marine habitats include oceans, coral reefs, and estuaries, where rivers meet the sea. The oceans are the largest of all habitats. Different species are found in the intertidal zone (where sea meets land), open ocean, and deeper ocean. Some living things in the marine environment create their own habitats, such as corals and kelp (seaweed).

Flocks of flamingos feed in the shallow water of this lagoon in Namibia, Africa.

An intertidal habitat is alternately wet and dry, depending on the tide. Things that live here, such as kelp and mussels, need to survive in both water and air. They provide food for other animals, such as this baboon.

MAP MASTERS

It's difficult and expensive to explore the depths of the ocean, so underwater maps are usually made using sonar. You might think modern mapmakers have charted every part of the world, but incredibly more than 80 percent of the ocean is unexplored and unmapped.

FRESHWATER HABITATS

Freshwater is water that is not salty. Ponds and lakes are areas of freshwater – they can be very small or cover thousands of square miles. Streams and rivers are flowing water that moves in one direction. Different parts of a lake or river make different kinds of habitats. For example, trout prefer cool, clear rivers and lakes, while catfish prefer shallow, murky waters.

WETLANDS

Wetlands are places where land and water mix, such as marshes, swamps, and bogs. Wetland habitats are very biodiverse, with a rich variety of plant and animal life.

Some plants and animals are adapted to live entirely underwater. Others, like this water lily, live partly in and partly out of the water.

MAPPING THE MEKONG RIVER

The Mekong is a river in Southeast Asia. The biodiverse habitats in and around the Mekong are home to rare and often newly discovered species.

1 FANTASTIC FISH

The Mekong is the second richest river (after the Amazon) in fish biodiversity and is particularly known for giant species, such as the Mekong giant catfish and giant freshwater stingray. However, hydropower development in the Mekong is a big problem for fish, blocking migration routes and isolating populations.

The Mekong giant catfish is critically endangered. Habitat loss and overfishing mean there may be only a few hundred left.

2 MEKONG MAMMALS

The Irrawaddy dolphin is an oceanic dolphin that also lives in rivers, but fewer than 100 survive in the Mekong. Other rare Mekong mammals include the smooth-coated otter, which is losing its wetland habitat across Southeast Asia, and the fishing cat, although this hasn't been spotted since 2000 and may now be extinct in the region.

The Irrawaddy dolphin lives in freshwater habitats as well as brackish (slightly salty) habitats near coasts.

FACT

AN AVERAGE OF TWO NEW SPECIES PER WEEK WERE FOUND IN THE MEKONG BETWEEN 1997 AND 2015.

3 TONLÉ SAP LAKE AND RIVER

In the rainy season, the Mekong rises enough to reverse the flow of the Tonlé Sap River in Cambodia and the lake expands, making a huge wetland area.

Tonlé Sap Lake is a biodiverse habitat shared by many rare or endangered plants, reptiles, mammals, and birds.

4 MEKONG DELTA

The Mekong Delta is where the river empties into the sea in southwestern Vietnam. The delta has a range of wetland habitats, including mangrove forests, salty and freshwater swamps, and marshes.

The Mekong is also vital for people, providing food, water, and access – the colorful Mekong Delta bustles with life.

GLOSSARY

adaptation the way a living thing is suited to its environment

altitude height above land or sea level

biodiversity the variety of plant and animal life in an area

carbon dioxide a gas made when things are burned and that people and animals breathe out

coniferous describes a tree that is usually evergreen with needle-shaped leaves

conservation protection or preservation of the natural world

deforestation cutting down trees and clearing the land

delta an area of low land where a river splits into several small streams before flowing into the sea

ecosystem all the living things in an area and how they affect each other

equator an imaginary line around the middle of Earth

estuary the mouth of a river where it meets the sea and the tide flows in and out

evergreen having green leaves all year round

extinct no longer existing, either in a specific area or in the whole world

fragment to split up

hemisphere the northern and southern halves of Earth

hibernation when animals pass the winter in a state like a deep sleep

hydropower (hydroelectric power) using the movement of water to make electricity

indigenous describes the descendants of people who lived in an area before people of other cultures arrived and became dominant

lagoon an area of seawater separated from the sea by a barrier

lichen a living thing in the fungi family

mangrove a tree that grows in salty coastal swamps

marsupial an animal such as a kangaroo or wallaby; the female carries her babies in a pouch on the front of her body

migration when birds or animals move to another place, often at certain times of the year

nomadic describes people who move from place to place, usually seasonally

peninsula a piece of land almost completely surrounded by water

poaching illegal hunting

pollution the act of damaging the natural world with harmful substances

semiarid describes an area that has little rain, but is not completely dry

sonar a way to "see" underwater using sound waves

species a kind of plant or animal

temperate describes a mild or moderate climate

tree line the edge of the habitat at which trees cannot grow

FURTHER INFORMATION

Books

Habitats (World Feature Focus) by Rebecca Kahn (Franklin Watts, 2021)

Living Habitats (The Big Picture) by Jon Richards (Franklin Watts, 2021)

Magnificent Habitats (Extreme Science) by Rob Colson and Jon Richards (Wayland, 2019)

Websites

www.earthobservatory.nasa.gov/experiments/biome
Investigate biomes, then test your knowledge at Mission: Biome from NASA's Earth Observatory.

www.bbc.co.uk/bitesize/topics/zbnnb9q
Find out more about food chains and habitats in savanna, tundra, and woodland areas.

gardens.si.edu/exhibitions/habitat
Take a virtual tour of the "Habitat" exhibition at the Smithsonian Gardens in Washington, D.C.

INDEX